Real Li★ves
Fearless
Women

Courageous Females
Who Refused to be Denied

Toby Reynolds & Paul Calver

BARRON'S

First edition for the United States and Canada published in 2017 by
Barron's Educational Series, Inc.

All inquiries should be addressed to:
Barron's Educational Series, Inc.
250 Wireless Boulevard
Hauppauge, NY 11788
www.barronseduc.com

ISBN: 978-0-7641-6886-4

Library of Congress Control Number: 2016959105

Date of Manufacture: January 2017
Manufactured by: Toppan LeeFung Printing Co., Ltd. Dongguan, China

9 8 7 6 5 4 3 2 1

Contents

What is a fearless woman?

A fearless woman is one who has challenged society's ideas about what women can achieve. Rather than accept the inequalities that permeate society, she has instead chosen to challenge them, her choices benefitting others and changing the way the world thinks. The women featured in this book are the frontrunners—they are the ones who took that first step, paving the way for the girls and women that followed them, and we all owe these women a huge debt of gratitude for how we can now live our lives.

But don't think that these women were never afraid. The women in this book were just regular people. What makes them fearless is their unshakeable belief in what is right. Perhaps they fought for years for what they believed or had to commit to one brave spur-of-the-moment decision, but either circumstance makes them fearless and worthy of our attention and respect.

Read on to find out about some truly inspirational women who heralded from the four corners of the world in the past 200 or so years. From the courage Rosa Parks exhibited in 1955 when she refused to give up her seat on a bus and the millions of lives that have been saved thanks to the tireless work of women like Marie Curie, to the more recent story of Malala Yousafzai, who almost lost her life because of her belief that girls deserve education just as much as boys, we should all be thankful for the contribution these women have made to fields as diverse as sport, science, politics and civil liberties, peacebuilding, fashion, art, literature, and music.

There have been many amazing and outstanding women throughout history, so this book can only introduce you to a handful. There will undoubtedly be many more to come who will inspire future generations of girls and women.

Rosa Parks

Born: February 4, 1913, Tuskegee, Alabama
Died: October 24, 2005, Detroit, Michigan

Rosa Parks was born in a time when African Americans in America's southern states did not have the same rights as white people.

In the 1880s, a number of laws known as Jim Crow Laws had been passed to segregate, meaning to keep apart, black and white people in public places. This included trains and buses, and public restrooms and restaurants. These segregation laws were supposed to treat different races as "separate but equal," and in doing so satisfy the Fourteenth Amendment to the U.S. Constitution that guaranteed equal protection and rights under law to all citizens, but in practice, this did not happen.

As a young schoolgirl, Rosa used to watch the white children go to school on a bus, while she and her black friends had to walk. She said, "The bus was among the first ways I realized there was a black world and a white world." This awareness increasingly bothered her, so in December 1943, she became active in the Civil Rights Movement, and joined the National Association for the Advancement of Colored People (NAACP). Rosa was now part of a community of women activists who worked toward making a difference.

On December 1, 1955, in Montgomery, Alabama, Rosa refused to give up her seat in the colored section of a bus to a white person. She was arrested and charged with violating a segregation law by taking a white person's seat. Rosa's arrest sparked the famous 381-day-long Montgomery Bus Boycott, when the majority of the 40,000 African American commuters living in the city opted to walk to work instead of using the buses.

The boycott went down in history as one of the most successful mass uprisings against racial segregation. In the short term, it resulted in the ending of segregated buses in Alabama. In the longer term, it led to a national determination to end racial segregation, bringing about the Civil Rights Act of 1964 and the 1965 Voting Rights Act.

Rosa's actions did have repercussions. Both she and her husband lost their jobs and she received hate calls and death threats. Despite this, she spent the rest of her life continuing her fight for racial equality. Rosa's actions showed the world how one ordinary person with the strength to stand up for her beliefs could make a difference to so many people in her own lifetime—and beyond.

"Each person must live their life as a model for others."

Emmeline Pankhurst

Born: July 15, 1858, Manchester, U.K.
Died: June 14, 1928, London, U.K.

Emmeline Pankhurst was instrumental in getting women the right to vote, during a time when British women had no political voice.

Emmeline came from a family that had a strong political stance, which molded her own views. In 1879, she married Richard Pankhurst, an energetic supporter of female suffrage, which is the belief that women have a right to vote. In 1889, she founded the Women's Franchise League with her husband, and its aim was to win the right for married women to vote in local elections.

Following the unexpected death of her husband in 1898, Emmeline became even more dedicated to her cause. In 1903, she founded the Women's Social and Political Union (WSPU). Her two daughters, Christabel and Sylvia, also became members. This new organization focused on getting women's voting rights, using "deeds not words" to further their movement. However, the arrest of Christabel and another WSPU member in 1905 provoked Emmeline to encourage her group to follow a more radical and increasingly militant path. This included directly confronting politicians, holding rallies, smashing windows, and arson.

Emmeline and her followers became known as "suffragettes," stemming from the word "suffrage." Emmeline was very active in the group and was arrested six times between 1908 and 1912. She and many other members embarked on hunger strikes while in prison in order to make the government acknowledge that the crimes they had committed were political acts. The hunger strikes often led to the suffragettes being force-fed.

At the outbreak of the First World War in 1914, Emmeline called for the group's militant actions to stop and encouraged her followers to take an active part in the war effort instead—working in factories, for example, so that men could fight on the front. In 1918 a bill was passed that granted some women limited voting rights. They could vote as long as they were at least 30 years old and the woman or her husband owned a certain amount of property. A subsequent bill allowed women to stand for (run for) Parliament. Many believe that the work women did during the war was what led to the introduction of the new bills.

Emmeline died just one month before Parliament granted women equal voting rights to men.

Emmeline Pankhurst

"We are here, not because we are law-breakers; we are here in our efforts to become law-makers."

Malala Yousafzai

Born: July 12, 1997, Mingora, Pakistan

Born in the Taliban-dominated Swat Valley of northwest Pakistan, inspirational Malala comes from a family that is passionate about education.

The region in which she lived had a history of educating children—both boys and girls. This was unusual for Pakistan, which has the second-largest number of out-of-school children in the world. Malala's father, Ziauddin, an educational activist and supporter of women's rights, founded and ran a chain of private schools called the Khushal Public School. Unsurprisingly, Malala's early life was dominated by education and learning.

In 2009, the Taliban were starting to gain more and more power in the Swat Valley and were attempting to ban things like television, music, and the education of girls. Malala wrote a blog, using a pseudonym, for the BBC about her life under Taliban occupation, in which her views on the importance of education for girls became apparent. The blog brought her to prominence. It resulted in media interviews and a documentary for *The New York Times*, as well as a nomination for the International Children's Peace Prize. However, it also brought death threats to her and her family.

In October 2012, Malala was shot in the head and through the shoulder, while traveling on the school bus. A Taliban gunman boarded the bus and asked for Malala by name before firing three shots at her. After intensive rehabilitation in the U.K., Malala did eventually recover from the ordeal.

As opposed to silencing her, the attack attracted even more attention. Hearing her story, over two million people around the world signed a "right to education" petition, which pushed the Pakistani government to pass its first Right to Free and Compulsory Education Bill, ensuring free and compulsory education to children aged 5–16.

Malala continues to make a difference. In 2014, she became a joint recipient of the Nobel Peace Prize, making her the youngest ever Nobel Prize Laureate. She has also gone on to start the Malala Fund, which promotes education for girls.

In 2013, Malala released a memoir, *I am Malala*, in which she said, "I don't want to be thought of as the 'girl who was shot by the Taliban' but the 'girl who fought for education.' This is the cause to which I want to devote my life."

Malala Yousafzai

"One child, one teacher, one book and one pen can change the world."

11

Amelia Earhart

Born: July 24, 1897, Atchison, Kansas
Disappeared: July 2, 1937 (declared dead, January 5, 1939)

Amelia Earhart's remarkable determination, independence, and entrepreneurial spirit made her one of the most famous and successful pioneering aviators of all time.

Born in Kansas, in America's midwest, Amelia spent much of her childhood moving from place to place. In 1918, after graduating from high school in Chicago, she visited her sister in Canada, where she volunteered with the Red Cross. As a nurse's aide she tended to wounded soldiers—many of them pilots returning from the First World War—and spent most of her free time watching the Royal Flying Corps practicing in a nearby airfield.

Amelia's first flight was in 1920 at an air show in Long Beach, California, where her father paid for her to have a 10-minute flight. This made her determined to fly herself: "By the time I had got two or three hundred feet (60–90 m) off the ground, I knew I had to fly," she said.

Over the following months, Amelia took a number of jobs to save the money she needed to begin flying lessons with the pioneering female pilot Anita "Neta" Snook. On May 15, 1923, Amelia became the 16th woman to be given a pilot's licence.

In 1928, she was the first woman to fly across the Atlantic, though only as a passenger. Afterwards, George P. Putnam, a publisher—who Amelia later married—began to heavily promote Amelia through a book, lecture tours, and product endorsements. Although Amelia rose to celebrity status, she was keen to establish herself as a respected aviator.

In 1932, Amelia attempted to fly across the Atlantic. Her flight hit difficulties, forcing her to land in Ireland instead of France, but she still became the first woman to complete the journey solo. She won many honors for this, including the Flying Cross from the U.S. Congress. In the years that followed, she set many women's speed and aviation records.

In 1937, Amelia made a courageous attempt to be the first to circumnavigate the globe via the equator. However, her plane disappeared over the Pacific Ocean on the final leg of the 29,000 mile (47,000 km) journey. After extensive searches, she was declared legally dead on January 5, 1939.

Her passion, vision, and achievements in flying mean that Amelia Earhart is still remembered today as one of the world's most famous female pilots.

Amelia Earhart

"Women must try to do things as men have tried. When they fail, their failure must be but a challenge to others."

Florence Nightingale

Born: May 12, 1820, Florence, Italy
Died: August 3, 1910, London, U.K.

Florence Nightingale is considered to be the founder of modern medicine. Born to an aristocratic British family, she had a revolutionary effect on nursing that is still remembered today.

From an early age, Florence showed an interest in service to others, helping the poor and sick on her family's estate. This grew into a desire to become a nurse. At this time, women from aristocratic backgrounds were expected to marry well and not have a career, so Florence's family disapproved of her calling. Despite this, she completed nursing training in Germany, with the help of an annual salary given to her by her father. She later started working at London's Institute for the Care of Sick Gentlewomen. Due to her aptitude, Florence was promoted to Superintendent within a year.

The Crimean War broke out in 1853 and there were reports of British casualties being nursed under unsanitary and inhumane conditions in the Crimean hospitals. Florence was asked by the British Secretary of State to set up a nursing corps to take care of these soldiers. Just days after receiving the initial request, Florence had mobilized a team of 34 nurses and set sail for Crimea.

Shocked by the conditions they saw, the nurses set about cleaning the hospital with the help of some able-bodied patients. In the evenings, Florence would make her rounds, carrying a lamp. This led her patients to call her the "Lady with the Lamp."

Florence wrote about her experiences in Crimea, indicating that many deaths in wartime hospitals were due to poor and unsanitary living conditions. This was instrumental in bringing about reforms in the healthcare system. Florence returned to England in 1856 to a hero's welcome, which included a presentation from Queen Victoria and a large sum of prize money from the British government. She used this to establish a London hospital with a training school for nurses.

Thanks to Florence, nursing no longer had a bad reputation. She showed that trained nurses and clean hospitals helped the sick get better.

Florence contracted Crimean fever during her war work, from which she never fully recovered. Despite this, she continued to work from her bed, determined to reform the healthcare system. She died peacefully in her sleep at the age of 90.

Florence Nightingale

"I attribute my success to this: I never gave or took any excuse."

Marie Curie

Born: November 7, 1867, Warsaw, Poland
Died: July 4, 1934, Passy, France

Born as Maria Sklodowska, Marie Curie was one of the most famous scientists of her time.

Although her parents were both teachers, education didn't come easy to Marie. During the 1800s, higher education in Poland was reserved for men, and her parents had little money to fund Marie's ambition to attend the Sorbonne in France, where women were welcome to study. Marie was determined to have a career in science, so she made a pact with her older sister, Bronia: she would work as a governess to pay for Bronia's medical school fees in Paris and, in return, Bronia and her father would put aside enough money for Marie to attend the Sorbonne.

During her studies for a doctorate, Marie became fascinated by the X-rays that had been discovered by fellow scientists Wilhelm Roentgen and Henri Becquerel. She then began her own experiments, examining the rays emitted from uranium.

In 1898, Marie and her husband, Pierre Curie, announced their discovery of two new chemical elements. She named one radium and the other polonium, after her country of birth.

Marie was awarded a Nobel Prize in Physics in 1903, alongside Pierre and Henri Becquerel, for their research into radioactivity. After Pierre's sudden death in 1906, Marie received a second Nobel Prize, this time for her work in Chemistry. She remains the only woman to ever hold Nobel Prizes for both Chemistry and Physics.

During the First World War, Marie discovered that X-rays, or radiology, could be used to find out what was wrong with injured soldiers. She also found a way of moving X-ray machines on trucks from hospital to hospital. Because of her tenacious spirit, Marie even drove the trucks to where they were most needed, and trained people to use the machines. Her discovery and determination helped over one million soldiers during the 1914—18 war. Scientists eventually realized that radiology had the ability to treat cancer. However, this came too late for Marie, who died of the disease in 1934 after a lifetime of exposure to radiation.

Marie's legacy now lives on through the Institut Curie in Paris, which she founded as the Fondation Curie in 1920, and it continues to carry out pioneering cancer research and treatment today.

Marie Curie

"Nothing in life is to be feared; it is only to be understood."

Michelle Bachelet

Born: September 29, 1951, Santiago, Chile

Michelle Bachelet became the first female president of Chile. She rose to power, against all the odds, after successfully establishing herself in the Latin American country's political arena.

While studying medicine at the University of Chile in 1973, Michelle and her mother were arrested and tortured in a secret prison. This was because her father, a general in Chile's air force, had opposed the military coup that was taking place in the country at the time. The coup had brought Augusto Pinochet to power so, considered a traitor by the new president, Michelle's father was arrested. He was tortured for several months before dying in prison of a heart attack in 1974.

Michelle and her mother remained in prison until 1975, when they were released into exile. Michelle first moved to Australia and then to Germany, where she studied at a university and became involved in social politics. Then, despite all that had happened to her in the past, she moved back to Chile while Pinochet was still in power, and went on to complete her medical degree. She also joined a medical clinic that treated victims of torture, a cause that was now close to her heart.

After Pinochet was ousted by the government in 1990, Michelle became involved in more senior areas of politics. This led to her position as the Minister of Health for the Chilean government and then the first ever female Minister of Defense.

In 2005, Michelle was selected as a presidential candidate. After tailoring her campaign to focus on promoting women's rights, helping the poor, and recognizing the rights of the Mapuche people, she became Chile's first female president in 2006. Michelle had achieved her popular win by hard work, though the likelihood of a divorced woman doing so in a Catholic country must have been slim.

As president, she was praised for her handling of Chile's 2008 financial crisis and credited with improvements in childhood education and in raising people out of poverty. Although her four-year term in office naturally came to an end in 2010, Michelle was one of the most popular presidents in Chilean history. After three years as the head of United Nations Women, where she worked to empower women around the world, she was re-elected on a reforming agenda as Chile's president. She took office in 2014 to serve a second four-year term.

Michelle Bachelet

"Women's strength, women's industry, women's wisdom are humankind's greatest untapped resource."

Panmela Castro

Born: June 26, 1981, Rio de Janeiro, Brazil

Panmela Castro is a graffiti artist who uses her work to raise awareness of women's issues and rights throughout the world.

Raised in Rio de Janeiro, Brazil, Panmela often witnessed her mother and aunt being victims of domestic abuse and also suffered from it herself. After studying Fine Arts at the Federal University of Rio de Janeiro, Panmela decided to use her skills to condemn such abuse of women.

A law was passed in 2006 that made physical abuse against women illegal in Brazil. Known informally as the "Maria da Penha Law," it was named after a woman who was paralyzed for life after being abused by her husband.

However, despite the law being passed, many women were unaware that the law even existed and that they have rights. This was especially the case in Rio's favelas (or slums) where access to information was limited. Using her graffiti tag—Anarkia—Panmela set out to spread the message. Through her graffiti art, she began to raise awareness of the law, while also empowering women to speak up and share their own stories of abuse.

Another way Panmela promotes recognition of women's worth and gender equality is through a network of female artists she began, called Rede Nami. The collective provides workshops for women and girls, and employs graffiti and guerilla art as tools to promote women's rights. It also confronts issues like racism and violence, and uses social networks to spread information far and wide.

Panmela has been recognized through various honors for her work, including becoming a Young Global Leader for the World Economic Forum. She has also received a DVF (Diller–von Furstenberg) Award for fighting to improve women's rights. The DVF Awards were created in 2010 to honor women who have "the courage to fight, the power to survive, and the leadership to inspire."

Creating world-renowned murals, performance art, and videos, Panmela travels internationally with the aim of transforming the role of women in society. Her work is acknowledged globally for its artistic merit, its message, and its ethos.

As Panmela once said in an interview: "Art is how we can be influenced and be an influence."

"The pictures say: My life isn't just on a wall. Learn to respect me, hear my voice. I'm not afraid to speak."

Jamie Brewer

Born: February 5, 1985, California, U.S.

Jamie Brewer is an American actress with Down's syndrome who has become an international advocate for disabilities in the arts.

During her childhood in California, Jamie had an interest in performing arts from a young age. She began theater training in 1999 while at school, where she took part in musicals, dramas, and improvisation comedy shows. Her big break came in Hollywood, when in 2011 she was given a role as a young lady with Down's syndrome in the popular TV series *American Horror Story.*

Jamie has long been a spokesperson for the needs of people with disabilities. At the age of 19, she became the youngest person to be elected as president of the The Arc of Texas. The Arc's mission is to promote, protect, and be advocates for the "human rights and self-determination of Texans with intellectual and developmental disabilities."

After joining Texas's Governmental Affairs Committee, she worked to improve the legal rights of disabled people. Most notably, she persuaded officials to abolish the term "retarded" from state legislation, in favor of "intellectually disabled."

In 2015, Jamie made the news headlines when she became the first ever model with Down's syndrome to walk the catwalk at the prestigious London Fashion Week. Modeling for American designer Carrie Hammer in the show, Jamie was part of the "Role Models not Runway Models" campaign. In an interview, the designer, known for her women's professional workwear ranges, told *USA Today* how Jamie had been selected for "being outstanding and inspiring in her field."

Today, Jamie continues to develop her acting skills at the Ruskin School of Acting in Los Angeles. She has also been working with not-for-profit film company, Bus Stop Films, who supports film-makers from marginalized communities or those who have intellectual disabilities. Other organizations she works with include the National Down Syndrome Congress and the American Association of People with Disabilities.

Jamie is keen to see more authenticity on screen and finds it inspirational to be a role model for young women. She is seen as a representative of how people have their own voices, no matter who they are or where they come from.

"Young girls and
even young women
(see me) and say,
'Hey, if she can
do it, so can I.'"

Jamie Brewer

Margaret Thatcher

Born: October 13, 1925, Grantham, U.K.
Died: April 8, 2013, London, U.K.

Margaret Thatcher was the first British female prime minister and the longest-serving person in that role during the 20th century.

After graduating with a degree in Chemistry from Oxford University, Margaret worked as a research chemist, before becoming a candidate for the Conservative party in Dartford, England, in 1950. She attracted attention for being the youngest and only female candidate, and for the quality of her speeches. However, she lost twice to the Labour opponent before eventually winning a seat in the House of Commons in 1959. She rose to power, quickly climbing the political career ladder. In 1979, she made history by being elected as Britain's first female prime minister after a Tory landslide victory.

During her time in office, Margaret become known for her uncompromising approach to politics and her willingness to stand firm in her policies. She came to power at a time when Britain faced economic uncertainty. In order to control inflation and the trade unions, she raised taxes and privatized government-run industries. Margaret's leadership style and hard-line approach to political goals gained her the nickname "Iron Lady."

In 1982, Argentina invaded the British-ruled Falkland Islands. Margaret sent troops to defend the territory in what became the Falklands War, and gained respect for taking back British control. Just two years later, she survived an assassination attempt by the Irish Republic Army (IRA), when it bombed the Conservative Conference she was attending in Brighton. Despite the attack, she insisted that the conference continue, and condemned the bombers in her speech the following day.

During her third term in office, Margaret implemented a fixed-rate local tax policy, nicknamed the "poll tax" without consulting her colleagues. Protests and riots against the tax broke out across Britain. After losing the support of her political cabinet, Margaret resigned from office in November 1990. She went on to publish books, receive numerous awards, and to serve in the House of Lords. In the years before her death, at age 85, she shunned the spotlight.

Some believe Margaret's policies cost millions of workers their livelihoods, while others maintain she saved Britain from economic decline. Despite the controversy, she is mainly remembered as a woman and leader of unyielding self-determination.

Margaret Thatcher

"If you want something said, ask a man; if you want something done, ask a woman."

Billie Jean King

Born: November 22, 1943, Long Beach, California

Billie Jean King was the first female athlete in the public eye to admit her homosexuality, and she is known internationally for breaking down barriers to gender equality in sport.

Raised in Long Beach, California, Billie saved up to buy her first tennis racket at the age of 11. A year later when playing in a tournament in Los Angeles, she was stopped from posing for a group picture because she had chosen to wear tennis shorts instead of a skirt. From this moment, Billie knew she wanted to make changes to the sport.

By 1968 she had climbed her way to the world's number-one ranking in tennis. Over her long career, she would win 39 Grand Slam titles and a record 20 wins at Wimbledon, but her most famous competition was the "Battle of the Sexes."

This match took place on September 20, 1973, against Wimbledon champion Bobby Riggs, who had claimed that women's tennis was inferior and that he could beat any top female tennis player of the time. In one of the greatest moments in sports history, Billie beat Bobby live on TV, empowering women around the world in the process.

A champion for social justice, Billie went on to lobby for equal prize money for men and women at the U.S. Tennis Open in 1973. She also founded the Women's Tennis Association, World Team Tennis, and the Women's Sports Foundation.

Billie was pushed into the public eye in 1981, when she became the first woman athlete to open up about her homosexuality. Within 24 hours, she had lost all of her endorsements. Never one to back down, Billie nonetheless persevered with her career, and continued to play tennis until she was 39 years old. She was inducted in 1987 into the International Tennis Hall of Fame.

In 2006, Billie became the first woman to have a sports venue named after her—the Billie Jean King National Tennis Center in New York. Her awards are numerous, including the Presidential Medal of Freedom, which was presented to her by President Obama in 2009. Seen as one of the world's most respected and influential sports people, Billie continues to fight for equality and social justice. In 2014, she launched the Billie Jean King Leadership Initiative, to continue her work of addressing diversity issues around the world.

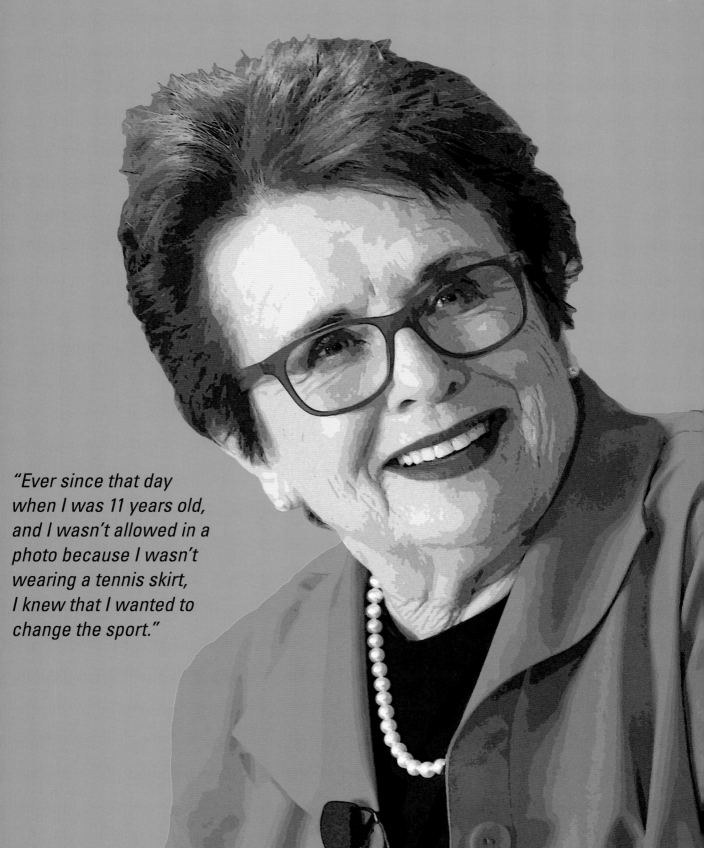

Billie Jean King

"Ever since that day when I was 11 years old, and I wasn't allowed in a photo because I wasn't wearing a tennis skirt, I knew that I wanted to change the sport."

Virginia McKenna

Born: June 7, 1931, London, U.K.

Virginia McKenna is an actress who is famous for her work in wildlife conservation.

Coming from a family with a theatrical background, Virginia's career in theater and cinema came naturally to her. But while acting in the 1966 box office hit *Born Free* with her husband Bill Travers, her life changed forever. The film was about a couple raising an orphaned lion cub in Kenya and releasing it back into the wild. It won acclaim and altered the public's perception of the relationship between humans and animals. The experience affected Virginia and Bill so much that they went on to form a wildlife documentary film company and to dedicate themselves to wildlife causes.

One of their new company's most famous films was *Christian the Lion*, but a more influential film, especially for Virginia, was *An Elephant Called Slowly*. While filming in Kenya, they came to know the elephant calf character, Pole Pole. However, when filming was over, Pole Pole was snatched by the Kenyan government and given to the London Zoo as a gift. Virginia and Bill did everything they could to prevent the calf from being sent away, including offering to buy the elephant themselves, but to no avail.

When Virginia and Bill went to visit Pole Pole in London, they saw how frustrated the calf was. In 1983, at just 16, Pole Pole died prematurely. To prevent anything similar from happening again, Virginia and Bill set up the Zoo Check Campaign, which continues to work to prevent captive animal suffering. This led to the formation of the Born Free Foundation in 1991. This international wildlife charity protects threatened species in the wild.

Virginia and Bill's charity efforts through the Born Free Foundation have resulted in the revolutionary reorganization and enlightenment about how zoos are run around the world. However, Virginia believes that there is still much more to be done. Since Bill's death in 1994, she has campaigned tirelessly to change laws and to close badly operated zoos. She is committed to the Born Free cause and regularly travels with her son and CEO of the foundation, Will, to fight to free tortured animals.

In 2004, Virginia was awarded an Order of the British Empire (OBE) for her services to wildlife conservation. She continues to make appearances in stage performances, although her focus firmly remains on animal welfare and related issues.

Virginia McKenna

"I cling to the beauty and strength of nature and all wild creatures with a passion born of certainty that only through them can I retain my perspective about life and my own part in it."

29

Winnie Mandela

Born: September 26, 1936, Bizana, South Africa

Born Nomzamo Winifred Madikizela, Winnie Mandela is a controversial public figure and is known for her battle against apartheid, or racial segregation, in South Africa.

Winnie had a background in social work and international relations when she met Nelson Mandela in the 1950s. At the time, he was the leader of the African National Congress (ANC), which aimed to end apartheid, and to give voting rights to black and mixed-race South Africans.

They married in 1958 but by 1964 Nelson was serving life imprisonment for accusations of sabotage against the South African government.

Committed to the same cause, Winnie took on the role of opposing apartheid herself, emerging as a symbol of the ANC's continued struggle against racial segregation. Despite being arrested on numerous occasions, leading to over a year of solitary confinement and torture in prison, Winnie continued her activism. She campaigned for equal rights and rebelled against the oppression of the government. Although put under house arrest in 1977, she kept speaking out.

Winnie forged a political career over the years, through roles as South Africa's Deputy Minister of Arts, Culture, Science and Technology, and as president of the ANC's Women's League.

Although admired by many for her commitment to the ANC's cause, the lengths to which Winnie would go to liberate South Africans from apartheid were extremely controversial. In 1986, Winnie made an infamous speech, supporting the practice of "necklacing." This cruel practice involved executing people believed to have collaborated with the apartheid government.

Winnie was convicted of numerous cases of kidnapping, fraud, theft, and gross violations of human rights, which led to her resignation from many of her positions of power.

In 1990, Nelson was freed from prison. The couple divorced in 1992 and Nelson went on to be elected president of South Africa in 1994. Winnie remained a close friend until Nelson's death in 2013. Despite the controversies, Winnie is an inspiration for many and is a symbol of the political goals of the black people of South Africa.

Winnie Mandela

"I am the product of the masses of my country and the product of my enemy."

Maya Angelou

Born: April 4, 1928, St. Louis, Missouri
Died: May 28, 2014, Winston-Salem, North Carolina

Maya Angelou was a multi-talented poet, author, actress, and dancer, who is best known for her biographical works.

Raised in St. Louis, a city on the Mississippi River, Maya did not have an easy childhood. Her parents separated when she was young, so she and her brother lived with their grandmother. At the age of seven, Maya was attacked by her mother's boyfriend. He was then murdered for the crime, possibly by Maya's uncles seeking revenge. The young girl was traumatized by the experience and became mute for years, believing it was her "voice" that had killed him. During the years of silence, Maya began to listen and observe the world around her, growing fascinated with literature.

After studying dance and acting at the California Labor School, Maya's early career was spent as a performer. She later moved to New York, where she concentrated on her writing career. On meeting civil rights leader Martin Luther King, Jr., she became involved in politics as a civil rights fundraiser. She would eventually form the Organization of Afro-American Unity with Malcolm X, a human rights activist, before his assassination in 1965.

After being encouraged to write about her life, Maya's most famous piece of work was published in 1969: her memoir, *I Know Why the Caged Bird Sings*. The work became the first non-fiction bestseller by an African American woman at a time when black female authors were very much marginalized. Despite attempts by American libraries to ban her work—due to its depictions of sex and violence—it is believed that it helped lead the way for black feminist writing in the 1970s.

Maya went on to produce many memoirs during her career, as well as collections of poetry, screenplays, and even cookbooks. Her most famous poem, "On the Pulse of Morning," was written for and recited at President Bill Clinton's inaugural ceremony in 1993. Over her lifetime, Maya earned 50 honorary degrees and numerous awards, including the National Medal of Arts in 2000 and the Presidential Medal of Freedom in 2011.

Maya became a respected spokesperson for black women and was considered the "black woman's poet laureate." After her death in 2014, President Barack Obama referred to her as "a brilliant writer, a fierce friend, and a truly phenomenal woman."

Grace Darling

Born: November 24, 1815, Bamburgh, U.K.
Died: October 20, 1842, Bamburgh, U.K.

Grace Darling is a celebrated heroine from the 1800s, who risked her life to save the survivors of a ship wrecked off an English coast.

Grace grew up in Northumberland in northeast England. Her father, William, was a lighthouse keeper, who took care of the lighthouses on the Farne Islands. Grace first lived with her family at Brownsman Lighthouse and later at Longstone Lighthouse. She spent her days studying, cleaning, and helping her father look after the lighthouse, taking her turn to watch the sea.

At 4:45 in the morning, on September 7, 1838, Grace was watching the sea from the upstairs window of Longstone Lighthouse when she spotted a shipwreck on a nearby rocky island. It was the wreck of SS *Forfarshire*, a paddle steamship traveling from Hull to Dundee. The ship had run aground on the rocks and broken in half. One of the halves had sunk during the night, with the other half now stuck on the rocks. Grace ran to her telescope in order to search for survivors, but wasn't able to see through the darkness until light broke at 7:00 a.m. When she spotted survivors, Grace and her father decided to rescue them.

Through gale-force winds and high tides, Grace and William rowed the 1 mile (1.5 km) out to the survivors, before making a second trip to rescue more. In total, 18 people survived the wreck, out of the 60 or so passengers and crew on board.

The news of Grace's extraordinary bravery and virtue made front-page news and she became the nation's heroine. She and her father were awarded medals of bravery. Queen Victoria heard of the rescue and gave the family money, while others also donated money and gifts. Grace received offers of marriage, and artists traveled to the islands to paint this brave woman. She became immortalized through plays, songs, and poetry.

Grace sadly died of tuberculosis just four years later, at the age of 26. However, she is remembered as a symbol of female courage and bravery.

A lifeboat in northern England has been named after Grace and the Royal National Lifeboat Institution (RNLI) founded the Grace Darling Museum on the 100th anniversary of the rescue. The RNLI continue to use her legacy to promote maritime safety and their work on Britain's seas.

"The cries of the sufferers on the remaining part of the wreck were heard during the night."

Benazir Bhutto

Born: June 21, 1953, Karachi, Pakistan
Died: December 27, 2007, Rawalpindi, Pakistan

Benazir Bhutto was Pakistan's first female prime minister, the only female to hold office twice and the first female to head an Islamic nation.

Benazir was the eldest child of the founder and leader of the Pakistan People's Party (PPP), Zulfikar Ali Bhutto, who became prime minister of Pakistan in 1973. Benazir had three siblings.

After studying at Harvard University in the U.S. and Oxford University in the U.K., Benazir returned to Pakistan in 1977 to tragedy. Her father was hanged after a military coup, so Benazir took over as leader of the PPP. Then, only two years later, one of her brothers was killed, thought to have been poisoned in his apartment.

Benazir persevered to lead the PPP, and, in 1988, was elected prime minister, becoming the first female to head an Islamic nation. During her time in office, she promoted industrial development and growth and implemented awareness campaigns to encourage women to become educated. She also developed innovative schemes to distribute money to Pakistani families in a way that empowered the woman in the family, instead of the man.

Although Benazir attracted admiration for her political skills, Pakistan's president at the time dismissed her government after just two years, based on allegations of corruption. She was reinstated as the prime minister in 1993, but her government was again dismissed in 1996.

In 1998, Benazir went into exile in Dubai and London, facing corruption charges that were later thrown out. She was allowed back into Pakistan in 2007, and was a leading candidate for the next general election. However, after leaving a PPP rally on December 27 of that year, she was assassinated in a suicide bombing. She left behind three children and her husband, Asif Ali Zardari. When the PPP won the election, he became prime minister.

Although Benazir's legacy is controversial, many women of Pakistan see her as an inspiration. She had established an Institute of Science and Technology in her father's name before her death, which young women attend today. She pursued an ideal that women's expectations should exceed running a house and serving the family, and instead show that they can serve the nation as educated and empowered people.

Benazir Bhutto

"Courage and grace in the face of adversity are the hallmarks of a great leader."

Marie Stopes

Born: October 15, 1880, Edinburgh, U.K.
Died: October 2, 1958, Dorking, U.K.

Marie Stopes was a scientist and a leader in the field of family planning.

After studying Botany and Geology at universities in London and Munich, Marie became the first female to join Manchester's science faculty. She went on to carry out scientific research and publish successful papers and books.

In 1918, Marie published a book, called *Married Love,* about the way she thought marriage should work. Her views in the book, in which she suggested ideas for preventing pregnancy and gave many tips, were considered controversial at the time. However, they ultimately helped to change Victorian attitudes towards marriage. Even though her views were initially condemned by the church and medical professions at first, the book was very successful—selling 2,000 copies in just two weeks. Follow-ups to the book were soon published.

Given that many families at this time were forced into poverty because they were unable to feed a growing family, women would write asking for Marie's advice. Marie was opposed to abortion but encouraged the use of contraception.

Having experienced an earlier marriage breakdown, Marie got married for a second time to Humphrey Verdon Roe in 1918. He jointly founded the first birth control clinic with Marie in 1921, in London. The clinic offered free advice to women, while also gathering data. By 1930, many other clinics had opened around the country. They became the network later called the Family Planning Association.

Marie was a leading advocate for birth control and was openly condemned by the Catholic Church for her views. In 1923, she was involved in a lawsuit with a Roman Catholic doctor, Halliday Sutherland, who had attacked her opinions in a book called *Birth Control.* She lost the case, but it did bring more publicity to Marie's cause. Her conflict with the church endured for most of Marie's life.

Marie spent a great deal of time campaigning for women to have improved access to birth control. Her work served to empower women and change prevailing attitudes towards contraception, making it more freely available. Marie died from breast cancer at the age of 78, but the charity Marie Stopes International continues her family planning work around the world.

Marie Stopes

"People who know the truth have no business to allow the powers of darkness to silence them on any point that matters."

Sister Rosetta Tharpe

Born: March 20, 1915, Cotton Plant, Arkansas
Died: October 9, 1973, Philadelphia, Pennsylvania

Sister Rosetta Tharpe was a singer, songwriter, and guitarist who brought gospel music into the limelight in the 1930s and 1940s.

Born to a mother of musical talent, who was a singer, mandolin player, and church preacher, Rosetta was encouraged from a young age to sing and play guitar. From as young as four years old, she performed with her mother on stage, and they continued to play together at religious concerts well into Rosetta's teenage years.

In 1938, Rosetta signed a record deal and released her first ever singles. Combining a blues sound with holy music, they were the first ever commercially successful gospel songs.

Rosetta quickly rose to fame at a time when female black guitarists were very rare, becoming the first performer of gospel music to take her music to the wider public. In 1938, she performed at the Spirituals to Swing concert in Carnegie Hall, New York. This proved to be a highly controversial move. Those in religious circles frowned on a woman performing guitar music, let alone performing gospel music alongside blues artists.

Nonetheless, Rosetta continued to bridge the divide between the genres of jazz, blues, and gospel. She divided her time, playing in churches and in secular clubs, and eventually collaborated with a blues pianist of the time, Sammy Price. When she again faced criticism from the religious community, she decided to team up with gospel singer Marie Knight to create more religious music throughout the 1940s.

However, both Rosetta and Marie faced the criticism of the Christian community once more in 1953, when they produced a blues album together. Their popularity as artists never fully recovered, and the duet split up. Rosetta spent the rest of her career touring in the U.S. and Europe.

Rosetta passed away at the age of 58, after suffering a series of strokes. Today, she is remembered as a groundbreaking artist who brought two diverse musical genres together to make a new sound, and as an artist who defied the norms to bring her passions to the stage. Her music influenced such artists as Chuck Berry, Elvis Presley, and Eric Clapton and, in 2007, she was inducted posthumously into the Blues Hall of Fame.

Sister Rosetta Tharpe

"She was the only lady I know that would pick a guitar and the men would stand back."

—Inez Andrews, in *Premier Guitar Magazine*

Jane Addams

Born: September 6, 1860, Cedarville, Illinois
Died: May 21, 1935, Chicago, Illinois

Jane Addams was a pioneering social worker, who created the first settlement house in the U.S.

Jane graduated from the Rockford Female Seminary in Illinois, in 1881. Like most women of the time, her prospects after graduation were very limited. Although she attempted to study medicine, she was unable to complete the course due to ill health, and she spent many years considering what to do with her life. Eventually, she decided to travel through Europe with an old classmate, Ellen Starr.

During their trip, Jane visited Toynbee Hall, a settlement house in London. In the 19th century, settlement houses were institutions that provided services to the community and aimed to bridge the gap between the rich and poor. Jane became interested in addressing the needs of people living in poverty and planned to set up a settlement house in an underprivileged area of Chicago.

In 1889, Jane and Ellen set up Hull House. They raised money, cared for the sick, and catered for the community through such services as a public kitchen and an employment bureau. Jane became a role model for the people who came from all over the world to live and work at Hull House. Residents started up numerous projects and initiatives, from sports and theater programs to campaigning for better legislation for child labor, factory working conditions, and school attendance.

Throughout her life, Jane was an advocate for world peace. In 1915, she became chairman of the Women's Peace Party and tirelessly fought to prevent the First World War. She campaigned for a peaceful solution to the war and organized efforts to provide food and relief to those affected. She helped found the Women's International League for Peace and Freedom in 1919 that continues to campaign for peace and political, economic, and social justice. In 1931, she was awarded the Nobel Peace Prize for her efforts.

Jane Addams is recognized as the founder of social work in America. During her lifetime, she published dozens of books and hundreds of articles addressing issues on social work, feminism and women's suffrage, humanitarianism, and world peace.

She died of cancer in 1935, but Hull House served the Chicago community until 2012.

Jane Addams

"Nothing could be worse than the fear that one had given up too soon, and left one unexpended effort that might have saved the world."

Madeleine Albright

Born: May 15, 1937, Prague, Czechoslovakia (now Czech Republic)

Madeleine Albright is a politician and was the first female Secretary of State for the U.S.

Madeleine was born in Czechoslovakia, but when the Nazis invaded during the Second World War, she and her family fled to England. She was a young child at the time, and it was only later in life that she learned they had left because they were Jewish.

Madeleine and her family eventually settled in Colorado, where she achieved great things academically, such as a scholarship to Wellesley College in Massachusetts. She was later awarded a master's degree and a Ph.D. in Public Law and Government from New York's Columbia University.

Her first stint in the political sphere came as a fundraiser for a senator named Edmund Muskie, who unsuccessfully campaigned for the presidency in 1972. She then worked for the National Security Council and various nonprofit organizations, while also serving as a professor of international affairs at Georgetown University. Then, in 1993, President Bill Clinton appointed Madeleine as U.S. ambassador to the United Nations—where she quickly proved herself to be a strong political force.

Madeleine developed a reputation as outspoken, promoting and defending U.S. interests. In 1997, she was appointed Secretary of State—a position never before held by a woman. It made her the highest-ranking woman in U.S. history.

In this role, Madeleine campaigned for human rights and women's rights around the world, playing a major part in various peace missions. She helped prevent the spread of nuclear weapons from former Soviet countries to such places as North Korea, and called for military intervention during a humanitarian crisis in Kosovo. Her term ended in 2000 when George W. Bush came to power.

Madeleine now serves on the board of directors for the Council of Foreign Relations. As someone who fled the persecution of war and went on to become U.S. Secretary of State, she proves that hard work can lead to great achievements—something she tries to instill in the minds of the college students she gives talks to today. In an interview with the *LA Times*, she said, "Encouraging young women to work hard, open their minds, and pursue challenging careers never gets old, especially when there are still so many barriers for them to break."

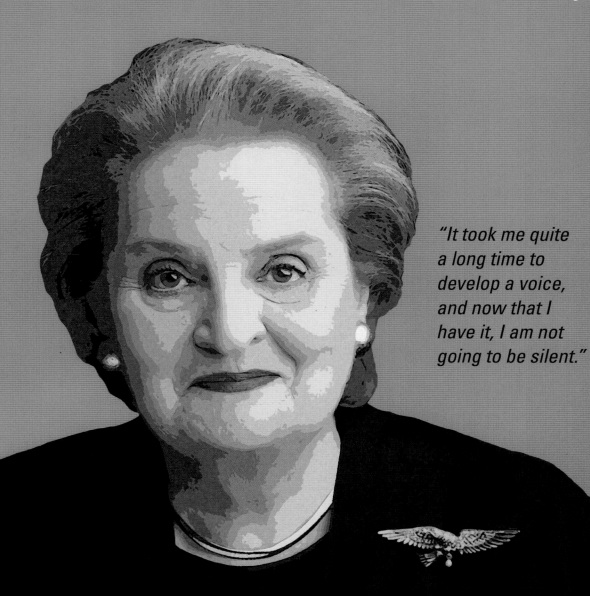

Madeleine Albright

"It took me quite a long time to develop a voice, and now that I have it, I am not going to be silent."

Valentina Tereshkova

Born: March 6, 1937, Maslennikovo, Soviet Union

Valentina Tereshkova is a Russian politician and was the first female cosmonaut to fly in space.

From an early age, Valentina was interested in parachute jumping and made her first skydive at the age of 22. At that time, she was a textile factory worker but had volunteered for the Soviet space program. She was accepted because of her 126 parachute jumps, as cosmonauts at the time needed to know how to parachute from their capsules upon returning to Earth.

Five women were selected from over 400 applicants for the Soviet's women-in-space program. This program was taking place at the height of the "space race"—a battle between the U.S. and the Soviet Union to prove their superiority in space technology. The 18 months of training included spacecraft engineering, experience of zero-gravity conditions, and tests to see if they could cope with long periods of time in isolation.

Of the five women, only Valentina was chosen for a mission. On June 16, 1963, at the age of 26, she was launched on *Vostok 6* to become the first woman to fly in space.

The flight lasted 70.8 hours and, although Valentina felt nauseous, she completed 48 orbits of Earth. The event was celebrated in Red Square, Moscow, by thousands of jubilant women and she was honored with the title Hero of the Soviet Union. Valentina's flight on *Vostok 6* was her only mission.

According to Valentina, the Soviet Union thought it too dangerous to send more women into space after her mission. She campaigned against this but to no avail. It was 19 years before a second woman, Svetlana Savitskaya, went into space.

Valentina later became involved in politics and was regarded as a spokesperson for the Soviet Union, for which she was given the United Nations Gold Medal of Peace. She remained politically active even after the collapse of the Soviet Union in 1991. When she married fellow cosmonaut, Andriyan Nikolayev, their daughter was of scientific interest because she was born to parents who had both been in space.

Today, Valentina's space capsule is on display at the Science Museum in London. She is still regarded as a hero in post-Soviet Russia and has received many honors and awards throughout her lifetime.

Valentina Tereshkova

"If women can be railroad workers in Russia, why can't they fly in space?"

The Maharani of Jhansi

Born: November 19, 1828, Varanasi, India
Died: June 18, 1858, Kotah-ki-Serai, India

The Maharani ("Maharaja's widow") of Jhansi, named Lakshmibai, was the queen of the Jhansi state in India. She led a fierce battle to protect it from British imperialists in the 1800s.

Lakshmibai lost her mother at an early age and was raised by her father in an unconventional way. He taught her how to ride elephants and horses and she became an expert swordsmith.

In 1842, she married Gangadhar Rao Newalkar, who was the Maharaja—or ruler—of Jhansi in northern India. Just a few years after the marriage, they had a son who died at just four months old, and the Maharaja passed away not long afterwards. As was common in Hindu law, Lakshmibai then adopted a son. This son would become the heir and would rule Jhansi when he was old enough.

However, British imperialists of the time, known as the East India Company, had their own laws to aid the expansion of the British Empire throughout India. They refused to accept the adopted son as a legal heir and instead decided they would take possession of the city of Jhansi. But Lakshmibai would not allow this to happen.

After first trying to regain her land in the British courts, without success, she rallied together an army of rebels to defend the city. Women were also given military training. Then, in March 1858, the British launched an attack on Jhansi and the rebels. Lakshmibai would not surrender, so war ensued. Her army fought tirelessly, holding out for two weeks against the attack. It is even said that Lakshmibai rode her horse into the battle with her son strapped to her back, two swords in her hands and the horse's reins gripped between her teeth.

When her army was eventually overwhelmed, they headed to the city-fortress of Gwalior. Again, they fought the British army, but this time, Lakshmibai fought to the death. She was just 22 years old. The British had succeeded in taking Jhansi and Gwalior.

Lakshmibai has become a near-mythical symbol of patriotism and honor in India. She fought fearlessly, leading her army in a battle against the unjust occupation of her homeland.

Many statues have been dedicated to the heroine and she remains a symbol of India's resistance to the rule of the British East India Company.

"The most dangerous of all the rebel leaders."

—General Sir Hugh Rose of the British forces, in his battle report.

Kathrine Switzer

Born: January 5, 1947, Amberg, Germany

Kathrine Switzer was the first female to compete in the Boston Marathon, paving the way for women's running to become a credible sport.

The Boston Marathon is the oldest annual marathon in the world. Until the 1960s, the 26-mile (42.195-km) length of a marathon was considered by the medical community and race organizers to be too dangerous for women to run. However, in 1967, Kathrine decided she wanted to compete. To this end, she had been training unofficially with the men's cross-country team while studying journalism at Syracuse University. She signed up for the road race with the unisex name K. V. Switzer.

When race day came, Kathrine took off from the start line surrounded by men, who were all supportive of her goal. But when one official realized a woman was in the race, he ran straight up to her, attempted to rip off her race numbers and reportedly screamed, "Get the hell out of my race and give me back those numbers!" Undaunted, Kathrine carried on. Although she had originally not signed up to the race with any motive other than to run her race to the finish line, she now felt determined to complete it for women everywhere.

Kathrine finished the race in 4 hours and 20 minutes, and photos of the incident with the official were broadcast worldwide. It underlined the hostility women faced for competing in athletics and raised Kathrine's profile overnight. From then on, she set her sights on creating opportunities for women in sport. This began with successfully persuading officials to allow women to *officially* enter the Boston Marathon from 1972.

Kathrine continued her career in journalism, writing columns and commentating for running events. But she also worked to improve opportunities for female runners around the world. Most monumental was a successful campaign with other female runners that resulted in the decision in 1984 to include women's distance races in the Olympic Games.

Her ongoing campaign to empower women through running has helped create a social revolution that was recognized when Kathrine was inducted into the National Women's Hall of Fame in 2011. Also a lecturer and author, Kathrine continues to organize races around the world. In addition, she is an Emmy award-winning TV sports commentator, covering local and national championships—including every Boston Marathon for 36 consecutive years.

"All you need is the courage to believe in yourself and put one foot in front of the other."

Fatuma Noor

Born: c.1987, Kenya

Award-winning Somali journalist Fatuma Noor has shared her investigative stories with the world, despite the many cultural hurdles she has had to overcome to do so.

Fatuma grew up in a Somali family in Kenya, and noticed as a child that there was a lack of female journalists covering the news of Somalia. She realized many stories were not being told and set her sights on becoming a journalist to tell them.

However, Fatuma's parents were unwilling to fund her journalism training, knowing that such a career would lead to threats and intimidation for her and her family. In a Somali community, women are not allowed to share their views in the presence of men. Even traveling anywhere without a brother, father, or husband is prohibited, and the existence of extremist groups in Somalia has restricted women's rights even more. Fatuma's ambitions would breach many Somali community laws.

Nonetheless, Fatuma pursued her career, achieving a B.A. in Communication and a diploma in Mass Communications. Her decision put a strain on her relationship with her family, which still persists today.

Fatuma's choice of career led to success, but not without further cost. In 2011, she decided to write a piece about men of Somali descent who were raised elsewhere in the world but would return to Somalia to fight for Al-Shabaab, an Islamist group. Out in the field with the recruits that she was researching, she was targeted by the Al-Shabaab militia for being a sole female traveling without a relative—a punishable crime. Held at gunpoint for eight hours, her freedom was gained only after a contact she had made in the terrorist group persuaded the elders not to kill her.

Despite her experience, Fatuma wrote a three-part piece for the *Nairobi Star* newspaper and achieved numerous awards for her journalism, including the 2011 CNN MultiChoice African Journalist award. She has also written exceptional undercover reports about such topics as underage girls from refugee camps being forced to work in a Nairobi brothel.

Such research requires Fatuma to take risks, but she remains passionate about her work. After winning the CNN award, she said, "There was a time in my life when I thought about giving up, but with this Award I'm not giving up any time soon."

Fatuma Noor

"I was told that I deserved to die—for being a female journalist."

Leymah Gbowee

Born: February 1, 1972, Monrovia, Liberia

Leymah Gbowee is a social worker and activist who is known for leading a peace movement that helped end the Second Liberian Civil War.

Leymah was just 17 when the First Liberian Civil War broke out. It brought with it fighting, rape, death, and brutality. After witnessing the effects of war, Leymah changed her ambition of becoming a doctor and trained instead as a social worker and trauma counselor, treating former child soldiers.

When a second war broke out in 1999, Leymah realized that if peace was going to come, it needed to be mothers who fought for it. So, as a woman of faith, she inspired Christian women to form a coalition with Muslim women and create a non-violent movement, known as the Women of Liberia Mass Action for Peace. Leymah led thousands of women in public protests to demand that peace talks take place. They eventually succeeded in forcing the country's leaders to meet in Accra, Ghana, to begin negotiations. At one point, when the talks seemed to grow stale, Leymah and other members of the movement linked arms to form a barricade, preventing the leaders from leaving until they had come to an agreement.

When guards came to arrest the women, Leymah threatened to take off her clothes—which, according to traditional beliefs, would have shamed the men. The stand-off was a success and, just a few weeks later, on August 18, 2003, the Accra Peace Accord was signed. It marked the political end of the war.

After making sure that the peace agreement was carried through, Leymah helped to coordinate democratic elections for a new leader, and the first female head of state, Ellen Johnson Sirleaf, was elected to power. Afterward, Leymah help found the Women Peace and Security Network Africa (WIPSEN-Africa)—an organization that promotes women's leadership in peace-building efforts. In 2011, she was awarded the Nobel Peace Prize for her role bringing about the end of the war.

Today, Leymah serves as president of the Gbowee Peace Foundation Africa, a non-profit organization she launched in 2012 to provide education and leadership opportunities for girls. She also travels the world to speak about women-fronted peace-building and gender-based violence. She is proof of what can be achieved when people band together across religious barriers to fight for the same cause.

"It is time to stand up, sisters, and do some of the most unthinkable things. We have the power to turn our upside-down world right."

Leymah Gbowee

Jane Goodall

Born: April 3, 1934, London, U.K.

Jane Goodall is a leading British primatologist and a UN Messenger of Peace who has carried out pioneering environmental project work.

As a child, Jane often observed nature and spent much of her time sketching and reading about animals. In 1957, after working as a secretary at Oxford University and also as a waitress, she saved enough money to visit Kenya. There, she made contact with a renowned anthropologist of the time, Louis Leakey. Even though she had no formal scientific background, with no degree to her name, Leakey was highly impressed by Jane's knowledge. He gave her a secretarial job and invited her to participate in field research.

In 1960, Jane began to patiently observe a group of chimpanzees in the Gombe Stream Reserve, Tanzania. At first, she was unable to get very close, but with perseverance she gained more and more of the primates' trust. She copied their behaviors and spent time with them in the trees. To this day, Jane is the only person to have been "accepted" into chimpanzee society. She prided herself on knowing the chimps as individuals, controversially naming them instead of numbering them.

Numbering was considered important in science for preventing any emotional attachment to the subjects being studied, so her use of names attracted much criticism. However, through her methods, Jane observed details unseen by others. She noted the chimps' complex social system and proved they ate meat—they were previously thought to be vegetarians. Her most outstanding discovery came when she saw a chimp use a blade of grass to fish out termites from a termite mound. It proved that chimps—as well as humans—could use tools.

Jane's years of fieldwork led to the publication of many articles and books, and she became respected in both science and the media. In 1977, she established the Jane Goodall Institute, which aims to protect chimps and their habitats. In 2002, she was made a Messenger of Peace by the United Nations and was also made a Dame of the British Empire by Queen Elizabeth II in 2003.

Jane's unconventional approach to research and her many discoveries continue to shape science. She dedicates her life to preventing the extinction of our closest cousins and travels the world to lecture about sustainability and respect for nature.

"The least I can do is speak out for those who cannot speak for themselves."

Coco Chanel

Born: August 19, 1883, Saumur, Maine-et-Loire, France
Died: January 10, 1971, Paris, France

Coco Chanel was a French designer who inspired a revolution in women's fashion in the 1920s.

Born Gabrielle Bonheur Chanel, she was abandoned as a child to a Catholic orphanage. There, she learned to sew and when she turned 18 worked as a seamstress for a local tailor. During a brief career as a singer in a café, she adopted the name Coco.

Coco developed relationships with a few wealthy men, who financed her interest in fashion design. By 1910, she had her own hat-making shop in Paris and soon opened boutiques in Deauville and Biarritz. It was in Deauville where she made and sold her first dress design.

Before the First World War, women's fashion was restrictive, with corsets and long skirts a staple part of most wardrobes. They were uncomfortable, impractical, and designed mainly to attract the gaze of men. Coco instead designed comfortable clothes that suited and fitted women's bodies, such as loose jerseys, trousers, and even suits—which had never been done before. She rebelled against the gender restrictions of fashion and liberated women from the necessity of restrictive corsets.

During this time, women wanted more practical clothes because they were working for the war effort as nurses and factory workers. Many types of material were in short supply and Coco's use of jersey—previously only used for undergarments—provided the comfort women desired. The 1920s were also a time of social and political change, when women received the right to vote in some western countries and were in many of the same professions as men. Coco's designs reflected these changes in attitude and circumstance. Two signature designs of this period were the "little black dress" (LBD) and the Chanel suit with its collarless jacket.

By the late 1920s, Coco's empire had grown to employ 3,500 people and encompassed textiles, costume jewelry, and her trademark perfume, Chanel No. 5. Other than a brief closure of her shops during the Second World War, she worked until her death in 1971.

Coco's designs remain popular today and helped change the way many women viewed themselves. By influencing the dress of working women, she empowered them as there was no compromise between looking good *and* feeling good.

"Fashion is not something that exists in dresses only. Fashion is in the sky, in the street. Fashion has to do with ideas, the way we live, what is happening."

Harriet Chalmers Adams

Born: October 22, 1875, Stockton, California
Died: July 17, 1937, Nice, France

Harriet Chalmers Adams was a writer and lecturer who traveled extensively in the 1900s.

At the age of just eight years old, Harriet had already embarked on her first adventure, traversing the Sierra Nevada on horseback with her father. With a taste of adventure deep in her veins, it was perhaps no surprise that she would become an avid explorer.

In 1899, Harriet married Franklin Pierce Adams, who had the same sense of adventure. They set off in 1904 for almost three years of travel through South and Central America, traveling by horse through the Andes and completing the rest of the journey by canoe or on foot. At a time when air travel did not exist and cars and trains were not yet commonplace, they completed a 40,000-mile (64,000-km) journey, visiting ports, plantations, mines, and native villages along the way.

Upon returning to Washington, D.C., Harriet proposed a lecture to the National Geographic Society—the beginning of her career as a lecturer. She wrote for the society's magazine, and the magazine's readers were surprised to discover that many of the most perilous reports had been written by a woman.

Harriet continued to travel, following the trail of Christopher Columbus across the West Indies and traversing through Turkey, the South Pacific, Asia, and many other countries. She became one of the first women admitted into Britain's Royal Geographical Society in 1913, but was not allowed to join the all-male Explorer's Club. In response, she helped found the Society of Women Geographers in 1925, and became its president. She also grew more involved with other female explorers and with feminist movements, promoting interactions between North and South American women.

In 1916, Harriet became the first woman to be allowed to enter the trenches of First World War France to document the battles for *Harper's Magazine*. While there, she continued writing for *National Geographic*, focusing on the experience of women. Upon her return to the U.S., she started touring and speaking to raise money for war relief.

Harriet is a notable figure in women's history for bringing together female explorers. She established herself as a lecturer and writer at a time when gender inequality made such things difficult, and inspired a curiosity about the world in others.

"I've never found my sex a hinderment [sic]; never faced a difficulty which a woman, as well as a man, could not surmount..."

Harriet Chalmers Adams

More Fearless Women

The women in this book are just a small cross section from the many fearless women there have been throughout history. In every corner of the world, every day, women commit themselves to brave acts, bold decisions, and innovative thinking. Here are some more fearless women:

Saint Teresa

Born: August 26, 1910, Skopje, Macedonia (FYROM)
Died: September 5, 1997, Calcutta, India

Agnes Gonxha Bojaxhiu never thought of becoming a nun until she was 18, which is when she joined the Loreto Sisters of Dublin. In 1931, she began God's service as a teacher in Calcutta, but her calling was not the blackboard but the slums of that city. From 1948 to the end of her life, she worked among the poorest of the poor, and her Missionaries of Charity continues.

George Sand

Born: July 1, 1804, Paris, France
Died: June 8, 1876, Nohant-Vic, France

Known equally for her writing and bohemian lifestyle, George—born Aurore Dupin—was a celebrity of 19th-century France. She discovered a love for the countryside and empathy with the poor as a child, and these were to inform her later writing. After a failed marriage, she headed to Paris and penned her first novel, *Indiana*, which railed against social conventions, notably the subordinate position of women. George enjoyed an illustrious circle of intellectual admirers including composer, Frederic Chopin. In the years after her death, she was remembered for her rural-based novels, but her true legacy was her undoubted inspiration for women fighting for their civil rights and independence.

Asmaa Mahfouz

Born: February 1, 1985, Cairo, Egypt

On January 18, 2011 Asmaa posted a video blog (vlog) to Facebook calling on fellow citizens to rally in Cairo's Tahrir Square to protest President Mubarak's corrupt regime and demand freedom, justice, and dignity. Her vlog is credited with starting a mass movement, and on January 25—National Police Day—thousands of Egyptian women and men gathered in Tahrir Square and in other cities. The Tahrir Square demonstration lasted 18 days, the army's use of force causing 1,400 deaths. Though Mubarak resigned, the military resumed a repression of opposition voices. Asmaa's plea awoke a collective consciousness for freedom, but the award-winning activist is far from free in her own country.

Indira Gandhi

Born: November 19, 1917, Allahabad, India
Died: October 31, 1984, New Delhi, India

As India's third prime minister, serving from 1966 to 1984, she learned the cut and thrust of politics from her father who had been prime minister. In office, Indira proved to be a strong leader, initiating agricultural reform to end food shortages, encourage exports, and provide employment. Her government's repression of a Sikh separatist movement led to her assassination.

Josephine Baker

Born: June 3, 1906, St. Louis, Missouri
Died: April 12, 1975, Paris, France

This African American singer and dancer was a phenomenon of 1920s Paris. Born into poverty, she began performing at 16. Successful tours led her to Paris and fame. During the Second World War, and by now a French citizen, she worked in the Resistance, earning the Legion of Honour and other awards. In the 1950s–60s, she traveled to the U.S. to fight for civil rights.

Aung San Suu Kyi

Born: June 19, 1945, Rangoon, Burma (now Yangoon, Myanmar)

Five years after Aung San's release from 15 years of house arrest, "The Lady"—as she is called—won the country's first openly democratic election in 25 years. After studying and working abroad, she returned in 1988 to find Myanmar in political turmoil. She organized peaceful demonstrations calling for free elections but, with the army in power, was put under house arrest. Though her party, the National League for Democracy, won the 1990 elections, the army refused to hand over power. Her 2016 election victory came with high personal and family costs, and in 2012 she finally gave an acceptance speech for the Nobel Peace Prize awarded to her 20 years previous.

Tawakkol Karman

Born: February 7, 1979, Taiz, Yemen

Journalist Tawakkol Karman received a Nobel Peace Prize, at age 32—and was the first Arab and only the second Muslim to be so honored. Called the "mother of the revolution," she was in the vanguard of Yemen's non-violent struggle during the Arab Spring of 2011 for human rights, especially those of women, and the movement for peace. Her activism was ignited in the first half of the 1990s when her country was torn by political instability and civil war, swiftly followed by the repression of civil liberties. Being imprisoned did not dint her zeal, and her campaign for justice and freedom continues, often from a tent in "Change Square," in Yemen's capital city, Sanaa.

Isadora Duncan

Born: May 26, 1877, San Francisco, California
Died: September 14, 1927, Nice, France

Isadora Duncan was the "mother of modern dance." Though her roots were in America, her free-spirited dance and ideals of beauty and humanity spread worldwide. Her programs, often performed bare-footed, revealed universal truths about the human condition. Her death was as dramatic as her life—her neck was broken when her scarf got tangled in a rear wheel of the car she was in.